For Marcel,

with love,

Marianne Polonsky

Climbing
the Shadows

Poems

by

Marianne Poloskey

Chi Chi Press

Maywood, New Jersey

Climbing the Shadows

Library of Congress catalogue number pending
ISBN 09640611-6-3

Chi Chi Press
P.O. Box 914
Maywood, NJ 07607
(800) 807-8265

Printed in the United States of America.

Cover and back cover photos by Lou Poloskey

First Edition

In memory of my parents,

Hans and Anni Koffler

ontents

Contents

The Egg-Timer

For his Sunday morning ritual,
my father deemed only the egg-timer
reliable enough to ensure
perfect 5-minute eggs.
He would turn the sand
into one end of the glass vial,
and show my brother and me
how to submerge the eggs
with a spoon, carefully,
one by one in boiling water.

The eggs would tremble,
their plump white ovals
hopping up and down
as if hurting
to get out, hitting
the bottom of the pot
with quick knocking thumps
gentle enough to keep
their shells from cracking,

while the sand trickled through
the vial's narrow neck
from one long blister
into the other,
balancing time
above gravity,
making time visible;
and we watched, entranced,
as the seconds sifted

past our eyes
in a steady thin thread.
We could almost feel
ourselves growing older.

And when the sand stopped
running, we were invariably
amazed at having allowed
five whole minutes of ourselves
to drift away while we
did nothing but stare
after them.

Never Again

All along they had warned
the worst would come at the end
of the war. Then one night ...

"One of your children will be shot,"
the Russian soldier told my mother,
"as our own have been shot."

His lantern came to rest
on me
and I stood up from my straw mattress:
a human shell
long programmed for death.

Blinded by the lantern's light
I readied myself:
my executioner had no face.

I thought of how nice it would be
to be free of pain
free of fear
of hate
free –
and I smiled.

"You are a brave little girl,"
said the soldier.
"You shall live."

I thought of how sad it would have been
never to find out whether
my father was still alive,
never again to kiss my mother,
play with my little brother or
hear my baby sister cooing –
and I broke
into sobs.

And the soldier joined
in the laughter of my tears.
I still remember his face.

Hate

I heard you tell
many a night, stay away,
but the door
was pushed open anyway
and the uniform
burst into our room.
I could hear you begging
in a little girl's voice,
but one boot dropped
anyway, then the other.
As, moving over,
you thumped
against the wall,
I felt an ache
in my shoulder.
And when the rhythm
of the assault
wired my feet
to your headboard,
I wanted to leap
from my bed
and grab the gun
he always leaned against
the door.
I wanted to shoot him
with his own hate.
I imagined
yanking you up by an arm
like a doll,
pictured us slipping out
of our bodies
as if they were clothes.

No longer targets,
we would float
through the window
into the wide-open
summer night –
bruised clouds,
you and I,
rising purple in the sky.
But I wasn't as brave as you.
I didn't even sob.
All I could do was
crawl deeper into darkness.
All I could do was flee
into sleep.

Years Hence

Every time I read of
war
children starving
I am once more
a little girl
skinny like her pigtails
shrinking from
her own shadow.

And when I see a picture
of a child
whose slanted eyes
fear has rounded
I find myself once more
staring
from a blacked-out window
into a bright-red street.

And then I wonder:
how many of *this* war's children
will be
as fortunate as I –
years hence
able to remember?

The Blueberry Day

Early that morning
Mother had sent us to the woods
to pick a topping
for the Sunday pie; berries
so blue as if all sky had crept in-
to their marble roundness.

By noon, when the sun's teasing
turned into attack,
we had enough
to go

home. But the trees,
whispering of royal friendship,
invited us to rest
in the pools of their shadows;
we plunged into their promise –
and ate our morning.

And our joy was of the undiluted
childhood kind: when it was done
our empty basket
was not stained with guilt.

The Sleigh-horse

Once, after a snow storm,
Papa ignored the dignity of his
policeman's uniform and offered
to pull us through the streets
of Berlin on a sled.

We whipped the air into steam
with enthusiastic shouts.
Faster, faster, fight the wind,
brave the snow, pull the weight
you made, go, go, go!

And Papa laughed and turned
himself into a sleigh-horse,
even neighing like a horse,
stomping his feet, slipping
on undercover ice, his night stick
drumming out its beat against
his struggling thigh.

On our sled-turned-throne
we accepted homage from
white-kerchiefed houses waving by,
from bowing trees, curtsying bushes.

And whenever we passed
a pedestrian we knew, we'd point
at our horse and yell,
"Look at us! That's our Dad!"

The Homecoming

. . . So I went home.

The safety of old friends,
of places strange in their familiarity
embraced me with pain-proof walls –
and I was lonely
for seas of freedom,
for wide horizons of adventure.

The oceans had been rough,
the skies intimidating;
yet, when I saw how time had narrowed
streets where I had played
and clouded childhood streams
I knew my memories would have to fade
before I could hope to find
all of the way
home.

Hurry, I said to myself: already
distant lands are changing.

Class Reunion

As I approach the long table,
all of them stop talking
and look up, like that day
in geography class
when I couldn't find Berlin
in the north of the big map
because I thought my home town
was in the center of the world.

Now, laughing, we reach
for each other across the years.
Long ago, we walked off
in different directions
only to end up in the same place.

We have returned to find ourselves
in each other's truth.
It's been the same
for all of us. We've learned
small things like
standing on both feet
to ease the pressure of gravity.

We are the secrets we promised
to keep, secrets long forgotten.
Life has marked our faces,
but we have stepped out
of our dreams to become real.

And somewhere along the line,
we stopped looking
for the enemy.

The Sparrow and the Leaves

One autumn afternoon a sparrow,
stalking through red
and yellow leaves,
suddenly became aware
that he himself was grey –
and bitterly denounced
the world's injustice.

Oh, sighed the leaves,
we'd gladly give you our colors
if only we could have
your wings!

Walking Lapka, My Sister's White West Highland Terrier

Maybe offering to walk her was
a mistake. Her little white body
strains eagerly ahead, pulling
the leash into a thin taut muscle,
as if to show me the way.
I give in, walk faster.

By the lake, fit smoothly
into surrounding hills like
the shiny bottom of a bowl,
I set us both free, and she shoots
down the path, a furry snowball.

She has no regard for a group
of dignified Sunday strollers,
who smile indulgently
while she untangles herself
from the maze of their legs.

She zips up into the woods, stands
on top of the hill like a lookout,
calls me with a sharp bark.
Then chases down again, making
dry underbrush crackle like fire.

I feel vicarious joy in her
exuberance, share in her delight
with freedom. When she stops ahead
of me and turns to lure me on,
I disregard my unhappy toes
and follow her to all the sights.

21

That Day You Came
To See Me Off, Mother …

… You waved your hand
so resolutely
as if to brush me
from your mind –
yet you smiled as though
I were just
arriving.

As the train began
to pull away
growing distance
brought us closer:
with drowning eyes
I memorized the poem
of your face,
read between
all those lines
I had not noticed.

Never had I seen you
look so small
nor so alone.
And all at once
I understood why
you wanted me
to go.

European Ritual

Sometimes
when a late breeze
opens the trees,
I think of summer
evenings in Europe,
how we opened our windows
to let the heat escape.

Everyone would lean
on their windowsills
like portraits of angels
propped up on clouds.

Across the street
we watched each other
watching day's retreat –

the sun swooning down
like a red kite,
houses stepping back
to keep from falling
into shadow.

But eventually,
shadow swallowed everything –
flowers, fences, trees –
even our window,
with us still in it.

At the Gate

As we say good-bye at the gate
Mother, you put my fears into words,
wondering out loud whether
we'll ever see each other again,

and I bend down into your embrace,
resting my face against yours
where I used to cry out
so many hurts, you reminding me

to be brave. It seems
I have practiced for this moment
all my life, yet I cannot hide
the sobbing of my arms

from your frail shoulders –
all the love I have ever held
telling me I must go,
must go.

Graveyard at Saarbruecken

In the afternoon our friends
take us high above town
to a tiny graveyard.
Here, soldiers fallen
in World War II,
German and Russian,
rest side by side
in earth's impartial peace.
Their statistics have been carved
into cloned headstones –
five lines of abridged lives
in an unrhymed poem.
As if elevating them
might vindicate the past,
the town surrendered
this plot of hill
with its long view of freedom
where now a grand house might gloat.
Reading the names out loud,
we consider our own lives –
what we would have missed,
leaving at their age.
We pick cornflowers
at the side of the road
and add blue accents
to each name.
Then we turn to go.
From the valley below,
pulsing in shimmering air,
we can hear the town humming,
cruising our ears like bees.

Two Ships Passing on the High Sea

Suddenly a ship approached,
a *fata morgana*
bringing us the world.

Dazzled by its white intrusion,
we rushed to the railing
and waved at the passengers

who were leaning so close
we could almost
touch.

For a still-frame moment,
the ship lingered broadside
as if to chat,

then belched a fog-horn salute
as it pulled away, going
where we had already been.

It shrank into distance,
and finally slipped
like a white stitch

through the seam
between water and sky.
I never felt so alone.

Lee

You promised us five good years,
and transformed the grounds
into a tangle of blossoms,

the flowers coming and going
with their different shapes and colors,
unerring as time: first the crocuses,

nosy and yellow, soon joined
by jittery violets making their
blue apologies for the long winter,

then tulips – red and yellow torches
whose conceit paled when the dogwood trees
tattooed the lawns pink and white.

How the garden glowed! It seemed to
expand in space as it grew
crowded with details of beauty,

each flower lifting its face to you,
to the gentle rain
from your watering can,

the roses halting their climb
up the lamp posts so you could
lash them loosely with string.

It always seemed to be summer – at least
summer is what I remember you in,
walking back and forth past these windows

pushing a wheelbarrow,
keys rattling on your hip, always
weeding or planting or pruning.

When you repaired the old cracked steps
stumbling up the hill, you etched
"Lee 1987 " into a corner, as though

signing the painting of
paradise you created
to wrap around your life –

your legacy to us. I should have known,
as you kept walking through
the remaining years, that all along

you were planning your leavetaking,
with every step going
farther and farther away.

The Old Widow

On nice afternoons she takes
her poverty to the park
where she feasts on the hoard
of her memories
and visits with the sounds
of her past
as her dog watches.

She marvels each day
that in all those years
nothing has really changed:
birds sing the same songs
out of tune but in tune
with nature; the sun fondles
her arms as gently as ever,
the trees still murmur
their eternal mysterious nonsense
and as always, the breeze carries
the ocean across the bay.

The honeysuckle has lost
none of its sweet perfume
(nor the rose which glows red
in her mind).

Lovers have not changed:
they giggle as they pass (hand in hand?);
a young mother talks with her baby
whose cooing mingles with laughter
of distant children.

She is all of them:
mother, lover, child;

but since no one confirms her
with a glance or a smile,
she is but a shadow in the dark;
and as she taps down the path
that her dog sees,
the roses burn hot
in her eyes.

Without a Word

Now that you have forgotten me
I have to remember
for both of us:
I am writing an urn
for joy deceased.

You left without kissing me
good-bye, without a word
of warning, without answering
the questions I meant to ask.

You have made the final entry
into the land of statistics
as a number
on pages of a book:
in tables, your death
is multiplied by those of others,
making it painless
to the reader.

Already, your name has fallen
to a hush:
what we failed to tell you
we have added to your epitaph,
like an apology.

Change

I love you
he wrote on my napkin
in his light hand.

Playfully I followed
the thin letters with
my pen to make them more
legible.

I love you, it now
plainly read, but
the writing was
no longer his.

By the Lake

It is quiet here, except for
the thin buzzing of insects
circling and circling –
fine threads of sound
that mend water and sky.

They belong to the lake
like the far-off blare
of a frog's horn, or the lovers
drifting past in their boat.
Stillness closes the water
after them like a door.

I hardly notice time
slipping away as evening
pours into the lake.
Slender trees turn themselves
into columns
to shoulder the dark.

With each breath
the lake seems
to shrink a little –
as if the water's rim,
flinching from the world,
were swimming back
toward the warmer depths
of its own blue center.

Garden in Autumn

The rain was tapping

needle fingers

on the window pane

begging, impatient,

desperate almost;

I put down my book

and lifted the garden

to my eyes:

grasses, flowers, trees

were drooping

with rain's pointed weight –

and all the summer colors

were running out.

Toward Evening

Toward evening the bulky sky
burst into flakes
that stuttered down
like so many broken promises –
endless series of curtains
gauzy with snow
pulling shut behind each other,
bringing dusk early,
and when the lanterns sprang on
in the courtyard, each flake
that rushed past them
carried a bit of evening.
Soon our neighbors started
coming home from work
hunched over like stalkers,
absorbed in the effort of
walking fast without slipping.
They fumbled for keys,
stomped their feet –
but once inside, they grew
careless, let the weighted door
fall shut with a bang
loud although muffled by snow –
then a long dark moment
held its breath
until lamp light lifted
the suspense from the windows.
After a while nothing moved
except for the snow
falling in its random fashion,
meaning no harm,
sealing us all in for the night.

Up Early

I see the grey
ribbon of dawn flowing
through the garden.

Fog still shields
the bushes' round sleep
while trees

push up the sky
and step forward to claim
their accustomed space.

In the grass, grown
long overnight, a brief
ripple of wind.

No squirrels yet,
but the first bird
opens the day –

        full of surprise.

Myrtle Beach, S.C.

For Ingrid

I always look forward to visiting you
in late March, to our afternoons on the beach
when we sit side by side in canvas chairs
as we used to sit in school.

You knit to the rhythm of our voices,
and I watch your capable hands conducting
the needles as they take bite after bite
from sky-blue yarn. You push the stitches
back in bunches as if they were
blocking your thoughts.

The sun does not yet have that
sting of meanness, and I can gamble
my virgin winter skin the first day out.
The atmosphere is charged with ecstasy
of spring. Sea gulls dive into the waves
like bullets, come screaming up,
having silenced their prey.

Little children are playing just beyond the hiss
of crawling foam, then suddenly jump up, stretch
to the horizon, train their voices
against the rumbling waves, pour the sea
over each other from red buckets.

My sigh dies between us in the breeze,
but you look up and smile at me
with the enigma of the sea;
and with every stitch you snatch
a bit more sky for your endless
yarn of memories.

Rifles and Roses

For my husband Lou

With your bayonet
you used to cut a rose
to wear
in your rifle –
a rose
the color of a heart.

Instead of firing a gun,
you played
in an Army band.

As I write,
someone
in another country
on another continent
may be
listening to music –
without realizing
what he owes
to a clarinet.

Writing

When you have gone, the house,
too empty for writing,
misses you. The red walls move
in and out like a heartbeat.

Like a child that invents
obstacles to going to bed,
I listen to the water plunging
through the radiator.

As the room warms, it begins to
smell dry, and I think of the desert
with secrets buried in sand
blond as my hair.

There, on a ruler-straight road
that stitches horizon to horizon,
a car would look as alone as the first
word I have put on this page.

By the time you come back,
I have spent hours
tracking years. Your approach
is as quiet as thought.

Behind barred sunshine
you are waiting for me
to turn toward you –
as if visiting me in jail.

For Your Homecoming

Where you are, near the sea,
only clouds distort the moon.
I picture you reading

by lamplight, becoming
the protagonist in your book.
As you get sleepy,

letters tilt backward
until you lose
the whole story to the waves.

For your homecoming,
I have changed
the covers on your pillows,

dried outside in the wind
which never fails
to bring the sea

to our garden. Tonight
the moon droops low.
Leaves brush against it

as the wind rummages
through the trees,
looking for you.

Picking Up the Pieces

I am cooking to jazz
from your tenor sax
until a sharp porcelain slap
stops the music
and the kitchen knife slices
red pain from my finger.

I find you apologizing
all over the livingroom floor,
picking up the pieces
of my favorite Chinese lamp:
the little hand-painted lamp
that has cheered me for years.

I cry, feel aggrieved.
You tell me how sad you feel –
as if you'd killed someone.

You collect the exploded
bridges and decapitated men
with their rust-red hats
in a paper bag, safely balanced
in your closet, one on top
of the other. One day soon,

you say, you'll spread your mishap
on the kitchen table and try
to fit the peasants back
into their accustomed setting
on the globe of their countryside.

By the time that happens,
I will have learned
some Chinese patience.

Cape May

We walk down to the beach
carrying our belongings
like refugees, and settle down
among stripes and polkadots

in the rented shade of an umbrella,
facing the bottle-green waves,
their crashing noise an excuse for us
not to talk. I start thinking

about the wind and the sea
and their strange marriage,
how powerless a storm would be
without the ocean's wide-open runway –

and how I'd miss the whiff of freedom
in clothes and pillowcases
that I sometimes dry outside
to conjure up childhood.

When it's time to leave,
I beat at the wind
that bulges the blanket
we lift up together, both of us

laughing now, loud enough
for the other to hear,
the way I heard my parents laugh
on summer afternoons

swinging me in the blanket
from side to side,
high, higher,
into the sky

but then, too soon,
much too soon
sliding me out,
to fold the day away.

Climbing the Shadows

We've stayed on the beach
too long, it's getting chilly.
I smooth a plot of sand
with my fingers, then get up
to go. It's only a matter of time
before salty tongues
will demolish the symmetry,
and I am tired of being
a witness to destruction.
You pull yourself up with a sigh
and follow me, the wind weaving
in and out, keeping us together.
The sun is only just sliding away,
and already I miss the light.
We climb the shadows back
to the house, you staying behind me.
By the door, you fall away
like a leaf. I go upstairs
to our room, which has never
seemed this large.
As I cross the carpet
to the wall of glass,
I don't care about waves
prowling the shore, or the sea
swallowing the sun –
what bothers me is
not knowing where you are.
Surprised to see you
sitting in your deck chair,
I am shocked by recognition.
Your face is turned up

like a hand. You are listening
for my voice, but I have no desire
to speak, like the times
I was so happy, I was sad.
Somehow, I cannot bring myself
to this immense darkening
using diminutives,
and if I call you by name,
you will think I no longer love you.
But now that I know you are here,
I have time to wait.

Leaving with a Heavy Heart

Leaving with a heavy heart,
the sun bleeds into the river.
Day's accumulated light
swims to the other side of the world.

Calmly accepting its loss
of sight, the river has nothing
to say. My cares
dissipate like smoke.

Whirring softly, insects
sew themselves into evening's veil.
Colors slip back into the earth.
Only grass still smells green.

Darkness rounds off the corners,
melting love and hate
without taking sides.
Night is a warm hand, leading me home.

Acknowledgments

Acknowledgment is made to the following publications where these poems first appeared:

Bergen Poets 30th Anniversary Anthology: "Class Reunion"

BP Links: "Toward Evening"

Garland Court Review: "The Sparrow and the Leaves"

Half-Tones: "Garden in Autumn"

Main Street Poets Anthology: "Two Ships Passing on the High Sea," "Picking Up the Pieces," "Climbing the Shadows"

North River Review: "At the Gate," "Leaving with a Heavy Heart"

The Rift: "Graveyard at Saarbruecken"

Route 80: "That Day You Came to See Me Off, Mother," "Without a Word"

War, Literature and the Arts (WLA): "Shout Loudly Through the Stones" (published as "Buildings"), "Hate"

Writer to Writer: "Writing"

"Haven," "Change," "The Old Widow," "Never Again," "The Blueberry Day," "Years Hence," "The Homecoming," "The Egg-Timer," "Lee," "Walking Lapka, My Sister's White West Highland Terrier," "Myrtle Beach, S.C.," "The Sleigh-horse," "Cape May," "By the Lake," "Rifles and Roses," "Up Early," "European Ritual," and "For Your Homecoming" were first published in *The Christian Science Monitor.*

"Garden in Autumn," "Without a Word," and "That Day You Came to See Me Off, Mother" were winners in the New Jersey statewide William Carlos Williams poetry contests.

"European Ritual" was the Poem of the Month on the Christian Science Monitor website during July, 2000.

47

About the Author

Marianne Poloskey was born in Berlin, Germany. Her po
have appeared in a variety of publications, including
Christian Science Monitor, *Paterson Literary Review*,
War, Literature & the Arts. She served as editor of the
Anniversary Anthology of Bergen Poets, one of New Jers
oldest poetry organizations, and has had frequent g
appearances on Fairleigh Dickinson University's r
program, *The Poet's Corner*. A translator and interpreter,
lives with her husband in Englewood, New Jersey.